A Special Gift

for my sister:

_____

from:

_____

date:

a little book of

hugs™

for
sisters

Inspiration for the Heart

HOWARD
PUBLISHING CO.

A Little Book of Hugs for Sisters
© 2000 by Howard Publishing Co., Inc.
All rights reserved. Printed in China

Published by Howard Publishing Co., Inc.,
3117 North 7th Street, West Monroe, LA 71291-2227

00 01 02 03 04   5 4 3 2 1

ISBN 1-58229-123-3

Messages by Philis Boultinghouse
Personalized Scriptures by LeAnn Weiss
Interior design by LinDee Loveland and Vanessa Bearden
Project Editor: Philis Boultinghouse

contents

1

a *Sister's* bond

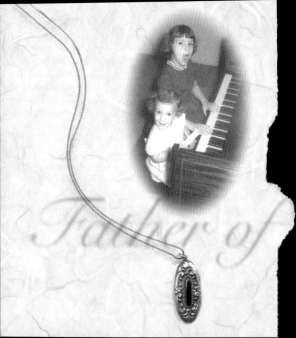

Father of

*L*et your soul be at rest once more. I've been good to you… delivering your soul from death and your eyes from tears. May you walk before Me in the land of the living. My supernatural peace, which transcends all human understanding, will guard your heart and your mind.

Peacefully,

Your Father of Life

—Psalm 116:7–9; Philippians 4:7

Sisters

*S*isters. There's something about the bond of sisterhood that is unlike all other unions. There's the shared femaleness— that alone is significant, but there's so much more.

There's the unreasoning bond of heritage—you're bound together just because of who you are. And there's the unrelenting bond of shared experiences—you've shared secrets and Barbie dolls, Christmas mornings and roller skates.

And then there's the inexplicable bond of shared genes and family secrets that make it so much fun to say, "You look just like Mama Lou when you say that!" or "Your lasagna tastes *exactly* like Mom's!"

$\mathcal{B}$ut this bond, this sameness, has a strange way of bringing our differences into sharp focus. And sometimes we can learn qualities or perspectives from our sisters that we do not naturally possess.

Take Mary and Martha, for instance. When Jesus came to their home, each approached her honored guest through her own distinct personality. Martha, the gracious hostess, took her responsibilities seriously. She cooked and cleaned and fussed and fixed.

*M*ary, on the other hand, took *Jesus* seriously. Everything else could wait. All other responsibilities were put on hold. The Lord was in their house, and she wanted to hear every word He had to say.

On that day, Martha learned from Mary that, really, "only one thing is needed" (Luke 10:42). On another day, Mary may have learned from Martha the value of a job well done.

*S*isterhood provides a safe place to learn new ideas, to explore different ways of looking at life. The comfort of our sameness helps us relax enough to learn from our differences.

When all the dust is settled and all the crowds are gone, the things that matter are faith, family, and friends.

—Barbara Bush

For when three sisters love each other with such sincere affection, the one does not experience sorrow, pain, or affliction of any kind, but the others' heart wishes to relieve, and vibrates in tenderness. Like a well-organized musical instrument.

—Elizabeth Shaw

2

a Sister's
love

*H*ow great is My love I've lavished on you that you should be called My child. You can love because I first loved you. True love isn't envious or boastful. It always protects, always hopes, always perseveres, and never fails.

My Everlasting Love,

Your God of Love

—1 John 3:1; 4:19;
1 Corinthians 13:4, 7–8

Sisters

Sisters are connected at the very deepest levels. Either she was there when you were born, or you were there when she was. Either way, you've been together from the very start.

*S*he knows about the time you told Mom and Dad that you were studying at the library with a friend. You know about the time she spent all her Christmas money on one concert ticket. She knows what makes you tick, and you know what ticks her off.

Such intimate knowledge carries with it great power— potentially dangerous power. But when coupled with love, it's one of the strongest forces for good in the universe.

The source of this vast power is the Creator of sisters. His unquenchable love is described in the Book of Romans:

"*N*othing can ever separate us from his love…. Our fears for today, our worries about tomorrow, and even the powers of hell can't keep God's love away. Whether we are high above the sky or in the deepest ocean, nothing in all creation will ever be able to separate us from the love of God" (8:38–39 NLT).

*T*he love we learn from God has the power to hold sisters together in the face of *anything*. The love of a sister can fly across an ocean in a letter and fill a lonely heart with joy; it can travel through telephone wires to bring courage to a weary soul.

25

It can pierce a hardened
heart and infuse it with
hope.

*N*othing can separate
those bound by the power
of love.

*Those who bring
sunshine to the lives
of others cannot keep
it from themselves.*

—James M. Barrie

a _Sister's_
comfort

God of

I am close to you when you are brokenhearted and crushed in spirit. Cast all of your worries upon Me, because I care for you. I, even I, am He who comforts you. I'll exchange your sorrow for comfort and joy.

Love,
Your God of All Comfort

—Psalm 34:18; 1 Peter 5:7;
Isaiah 51:12;
Jeremiah 31:13

Sisters

A sister, it seems, has extrasensory perception. When you hurt, she feels your pain. When you're happy, she shares your joy. When you're frightened, she understands.

*A*nd when a dark day comes, a sister's not afraid to enter into the darkness with you. She walks in—invited or not, it doesn't matter— and she brings with her the comfort of God. What she's really bringing is *recycled* comfort.

$\int$econd Corinthians tells us that God "comforts us in all our troubles, so that we can comfort those in any trouble with the comfort we ourselves have received from God" (1:4).

$\mathcal{T}$he comfort God offers
us when we're hurting is
recycled and used to comfort
the hurting heart of another.
That's what a sister brings
with her when she walks
into your darkness. She
brings the comfort of God
recycled just for you.

*A*nd a sister has a special
advantage when it comes to
the comfort ministry. She
can hear the hidden fear in
your voice that no one else
can hear. She can see the
masked sadness on your face
that no one else can see.

*E*ven when you try to hide your worry or your pain, a sister can often see through you, right to the truth.

*A*nd aren't you glad she can? Although she drove you crazy when you were ten—and still does on occasion—her keen perception sees who you really are, and she loves you anyway.

A sister who can do that—who can see straight through to the truth of you, who can be *trusted* with the truth of you—is like a "ministering angel" (see Hebrews 1:14) sent straight from heaven to you with a recycled hug of comfort.

There never was a heart truly great and generous that was not also tender and compassionate.

—Robert Frost

4

a Sister's
challenge

When you are pure in heart, you'll receive blessings and see Me. Prevent sin by hiding Scripture in your heart and living according to My Word. I'll give you a pure heart and renew a steadfast spirit within you.

Blessings,
Your Holy God

—Matthew 5:8;
Psalms 119:9; 51:10

Sisters

A sister can be pretty demanding. When you were little, she may have demanded to have your doll or her way or your mom's attention. But sometimes, now that you're adults, she might demand something else: She might demand that you be all God has called you to be.

*A*nd that's a good kind of demand—rising from a love that settles only for the best in you.

There may have been a time—or a time may yet come—when your sister had to come to your rescue, a time when she had to rescue you from yourself. A time when you'd lost sight of who you are in God and were swept away by something that, deep down, you knew was not who you really are.

$\mathcal{I}$t may have been a spirit of bitterness toward your husband or a heart full of fear about the future or a dangerous attraction to something that would cause you harm.

*N*ot many have earned
the right to challenge you
at times like these. Not
many have invested years of
being there for you, hours
of listening to your hurts, or
a lifetime of getting to
know you. But a sister has.

A sister has earned the right to "urge you to live a life worthy of the calling you have received" (Ephesians 4:1).

A sister has earned the right to take you by the shoulders, look you in the eyes, and say what needs to be said. She's tough, all right. But a sister who calls you to a "life worthy of the calling" also knows how to restore her sister with gentleness and love.

$\mathcal{S}$isters settle only for
the best that each can be.

For there is no friend
    like a sister;
In calm or stormy
    weather;
To cheer one on the
    tedious way,
To fetch one if one goes
    astray,
To lift one if one totters
    down,
To strengthen whilst
    one stands.

—Christina Rossetti

How could we endure to live and let time pass if we were always crying for one day or one year to come back—if we did not know that every day in a life fills the whole life with expectation and memory and that these are that day.

—Out of the Silent Planet,
C. S. Lewis

5

a Sister's
service

*U*se the gifts I've given you to serve others. Make love your motivation. I stockpile you with My all-sufficient grace, equipping you with more than enough for every good deed I've prepared for you.

Serve Joyfully,

Jesus

—1 Peter 4:10;
1 Corinthians 16:14;
2 Corinthians 9:8

Sisters

"Be nice to your sister!"

Sound familiar? With just a little bit of concentration, you can probably hear your mother's voice echoing back from…well, we won't say how many years…but from somewhere in the "not-too-distant" past.

*D*id you ever get tired of trying to be nice to your sister? Maybe, even now, she taxes your patience on occasion. Like when she tries to tell you how to raise your kids before she's even raised hers. Or when she is at your house as a guest and insists on setting the table her way.

*Y*ou have to admit:
As much as you love her,
you sometimes get tired of
being nice to your sister.

*B*ut there are times
when she really needs you.
And sometimes the need
goes on for longer than is
comfortable. It's at times
like these that we can be
spurred on only by some
other words from the distant
past, but these words carry
even more authority than
your mother's:

"*Let us not become weary in doing good, for at the proper time we will reap a harvest if we do not give up*" (Galatians 6:9).

$\mathcal{S}$omething about those words infuses the weary heart with strength and the ability to keep going:

*I*t's the acknowledgment
of the fact that doing good is
wearisome at times. And that
acknowledgment allows us to
feel that we're not alone in
our weariness and to know
that it's a trait common to all
people—even sisters who are
trying to serve but are tired of
trying.

And that acknowledgment—coupled with the godly reminder to persevere and the promise of future reward—gives us the strength and the resolve to keep on being nice to our sisters.